Options Trading Simplified

How to Generate Weekly Income in All Markets and Turn Fridays into Potential Paydays Using Weekly Options Strategies

M. D. Lloyd Ph.D

Copyright © 2024 by M.D. Lloyd, Ph.D.

All rights reserved. No part of this book may be reproduced, stored in a retrieval system, or transmitted in any form or by any means, electronic, mechanical, photocopying, recording, scanning, or otherwise, except as permitted under Section 107 or 108 of the 1976 United States Copyright Act, without the prior written permission of the publisher.

ISBN: 9798325960932

Publisher: M.D. Lloyd, Ph.D.

First Edition

Printed in the United States of America

Disclaimer: The information contained in this book is for informational purposes only and should not be construed as financial advice. The author and publisher are not financial advisors and make no guarantees regarding the accuracy or completeness of the information presented. Readers are encouraged to conduct their own research and due diligence before making any investment decisions.

DEDICATION

To all those who yearn for financial freedom and are ready to take control of their future,

This book is for you.

May your journey into options trading be filled with learning, growth, and the potential to unlock your financial goals.

TABLE OF CONTENTS

ACKNOWLEDGMENTS	5
INTRODUCTION	6
UNDERSTANDING YOUR RELATIONSHIP WITH MONEY	19
OPTIONS 101: Calls, Puts, Strikes, and Expiry	25
UNDERSTANDING THE MECHANICS OF BUYING AND SELLING OPTIONS	29
THE CLOCK IS TICKING: TIME DECAY AND OPTIONS PRICING	38
MANAGING RISK: Stop-Loss Orders and Your Safety Net	48
THE POWER OF WEEKLY OPTIONS: Strategies for Different Markets	57
COVERED CALLS: Generating Income with a Stock You Already Own	60
CASH-SECURED PUTS: Earning Income by Taking on an Obligation	72
BEYOND BASICS: Exploring Additional Weekly Strategies	85
RISK MANAGEMENT DEEP DIVE: Beyond Stop-Loss Orders	106
TECHNICAL ANALYSIS FOR OPTIONS TRADERS: Identifying Opportunities	111
THE LONG GAME: Recap, Realistic Expectations, and Moving Forward	117
APPENDIX	123
Glossary	123
BONUS	127
Practice Exercises and Sample Trading Plans	127
ABOUT THE AUTHOR	135

ACKNOWLEDGMENTS

Writing this book wouldn't have been possible without the support and inspiration of many incredible people.

First and foremost, I want to express my deepest gratitude to T.Y Smith who was invaluable throughout this journey.

A special thank you goes to my wife and children for their constant encouragement and belief in me. Your understanding during long writing sessions and your prayerful spirit kept me motivated.

I am also grateful to my editor, J.B Theophilus, for your meticulous attention to detail and insightful suggestions. Your expertise significantly improved the clarity and flow of this book.

Finally, a heartfelt thank you to the early readers who provided valuable feedback and helped refine the content. Your honest contributions ensured that "Options Trading Simplified" is a resource that truly benefits aspiring options traders.

To everyone who played a role in bringing this book to life, thank you.

INTRODUCTION

The Dot-Com Bust and the Dawn of Weekly Options.

Remember the year 1999? The air crackled with a new kind of electricity. The internet, once a clunky dial-up connection, was transforming into a vibrant world. News channels buzzed with stories of companies with strange names ending in ".com" – Amazon, eBay, Pets.com (yes, really, a company that sold pet supplies online). These companies, it seemed, were the future, poised to revolutionize everything from shopping to communication.

The atmosphere was infectious. Everyone, it seemed, was jumping on the bandwagon. Stories of overnight millionaires, people who made a fortune investing in these fledgling internet companies, filled the airwaves. Every email screamed "get in on the ground floor!" Every financial advisor seemed to be pushing these new internet stocks.

Caught up in the excitement, I, like many other young investors in Texas, decided to take the plunge. Investing in these companies felt like a sure thing. The future was bright, and these companies were at the forefront. Who wouldn't want a piece of that action?

But then, as quickly as it began, the dream turned sour. In the early 2000s, the bubble burst. Reality set in. Many of these dot-com companies had no clear path to profitability, their valuations were based on hype rather than fundamentals. As the market soured, investor confidence plummeted, and the tech-heavy NASDAQ stock exchange took a nosedive. Stocks that once soared to unimaginable heights came crashing down, wiping out fortunes in a matter of months.

My own portfolio, heavily invested in these dot-com companies, wasn't spared. The losses were significant, a harsh lesson in the dangers of chasing the next big thing without proper due diligence. Discouraged and disappointed, I felt like a fool. Investing was supposed to secure my future, not leave me scrambling to cover the bills.

Instead of giving up after the disaster, I went into serious research, reading books, taking courses, and hanging out with experienced traders. It was during this time of financial despair that I stumbled upon options trading. Admittedly, at first, I approached it with a healthy dose of skepticism. Could this really be a way to recover my losses and build a more secure future for my family?

Through research and careful exploration, I discovered that options offered a different way to participate in the market, a way that talked about potentially generating income, not just chasing the next big windfall. This wasn't about buying stocks and hoping for a home run; it was about understanding strategies and managing risk.

The dot-com crash may have shaken our faith in the market, but it also opened the door to new possibilities. This book, "Options Trading Simplified," is your roadmap to navigating the world of options, specifically focusing on strategies that can generate income on a weekly basis.

We will start by demystifying the basics - options terminology, mechanics of buying and selling options contracts, and how factors like time decay and volatility affect their value. We will also emphasize the importance of risk management from the beginning, so you can approach options trading with a healthy dose of caution.

Then, we will delve into the heart of the matter: weekly options strategies for income generation. We will explore popular strategies like covered calls and cash-secured puts, explaining their mechanics, potential profits and losses, and the market conditions they are best suited for.

By the end of Part 3, you will have a solid foundation in income-generating weekly options strategies. But that is not all! We will also explore some advanced topics, like the "Greeks" (delta, gamma, rho) that influence option pricing, and how to use technical analysis to identify potential trading opportunities.

Finally, we will wrap things up by recapping the key takeaways, reiterating the importance of realistic expectations and ongoing learning. We will also provide resources for further exploration, so you can continue your options trading journey.

This book is designed to be clear, concise, and engaging. We will use simple language and visuals to explain complex concepts. Most importantly, we will focus on equipping you with the knowledge and skills to explore the potential of income generation through weekly options trading.

Why Weekly Options Shine for Income Generation

While all options offer unique benefits, weekly options hold particular advantages when it comes to generating income:

Frequent Expirations: Weekly options contracts expire every Friday, compared to monthly options that expire on the third Friday of each month. This translates to more frequent opportunities to potentially capture profits and redeploy capital into new trades.

Faster Time Decay: Time decay (theta) is the enemy of options as their value erodes over time. Weekly options have a shorter lifespan compared to monthly options, meaning time decay works in your favor. The faster time decay can be beneficial for certain income-generating strategies where you aim to profit from small price movements before the option expires.

Potentially Lower Costs: Due to their shorter lifespan, weekly options often have lower premiums (the cost of buying an option) compared to their monthly counterparts. This can be a significant advantage, especially when employing strategies that involve selling options and collecting premium income.

Flexibility and Adaptability: The shorter timeframe of weekly options allows you to adapt your strategies more readily to changing market conditions. If your initial analysis changes, you can potentially adjust your position or close the trade before the following week, limiting potential losses.

Focus on Short-Term Movements: Many income-generating options strategies focus on profiting from small price movements within a short timeframe. Weekly options align perfectly with this approach, allowing you to capitalize on short-term market fluctuations.

Think of weekly options like 'mini experiments': You can test your strategies more frequently, potentially generate income more regularly, and adapt your approach based on market conditions with less capital commitment compared to monthly options.

It is important to remember: While these are some of the advantages of weekly options, they also come with increased risk due to their shorter lifespan and potentially higher volatility. This book will equip you with the knowledge to navigate these risks and make informed decisions.

Who Is This Book For?

This book is designed for individuals who are interested in exploring the exciting world of options trading, with a specific focus on generating income through weekly options strategies. Here is a closer look at who can benefit most from this guide:

1. The Post-Dot-Com Investor: If you, like many others, were burned by the dot-com bubble or other trading catastrophe and are hesitant to jump back into traditional stock picking, this book offers an alternative approach. We will explore how options can be used to potentially generate income without the same level of risk associated with buying stocks outright.

2. The Income-Seeker: Are you looking for ways to potentially supplement your income or create a new income stream? This book will equip you with the knowledge and strategies to explore options trading as a potential tool for generating regular income.

3. The Active Trader: If you enjoy the fast-paced world of trading and are looking for new ways to participate in the market, weekly options offer exciting possibilities. This book will guide you through various income-generating strategies that can be implemented and monitored throughout the week.

4. The Risk-Aware Learner: We understand that options trading involves inherent risks. This book is not about reckless gambling; it is about education and risk management. We will emphasize the importance of understanding the risks involved and provide the tools to approach options trading with a cautious and calculated approach.

No Prior Options Experience Needed: This book is designed for beginners with a basic understanding of the stock market. We will break down the complex world of options into easy-to-understand concepts, so you can build a solid foundation before venturing into the world of weekly options strategies.

What You Will Learn!

1. Option Basics: We will break down core concepts like calls, puts, strikes, and expiry dates, making options trading understandable and approachable.

2. How options contracts work - buying and selling calls and puts - through clear explanations and examples.

3. How time (Theta) erodes the value of options – a crucial factor in income-generating strategies.

4. How market fluctuations (volatility) impact option prices, turning them into potential opportunities.

5. How to set stop-loss orders to limit potential losses on your options trades.

6. A deeper knowledge of risk management techniques to navigate the options market with a cautious approach.

7. How you can explore the unique advantages of weekly options for income generation, including frequent expirations and faster time decay.

8. How to dissect popular strategies like covered calls and cash-secured puts and their mechanics.

9. You will learn concepts like delta, gamma, and rho (in simpler terms) to understand how they influence option pricing.

10. How to use basic technical analysis indicators to identify potential trading opportunities for your weekly options strategies.

In summary, you are going to learn:
- All that you need to know about Weekly Options to generate reasonable cash

- How to set up a complete trading account and trades with complete-at-night protection (no margin calls)
- How to adjust trades in all markets
- How to create a trading plan so that trading is automatic, not emotional
- How to make the money that you need and sleep well at night

NOTE: Throughout the book, we will emphasize the importance of backtesting and paper trading before risking real capital. We will use clear language and visuals to explain complex concepts, making your options trading journey informative and engaging.

By the end of this book, you will be equipped with the knowledge and confidence to explore the potential of weekly options for generating income.

WHY I AM WRITING THIS BOOK

For over two decades, I have been on a journey through the world of options trading. It is been a path filled with learning, refining strategies, and ultimately, discovering a method that works for me. That method? **Selling weekly options.**

The beauty of selling weekly options lies in its ability to generate consistent income. It is not about chasing the next hot stock; it is about building a dependable stream of cash flow.

Imagine this: the ability to **generate income from the market, with a focus on risk management.** This approach offers peace of mind, knowing you can potentially cover your bills and pursue your desired lifestyle, all from the comfort of your home – or anywhere with an internet connection!

Why am I writing this book? Because I believe this knowledge can empower others as it helped me recovered from the Dotcom disaster. This book, "Options Trading Simplified," is your guide to understanding weekly options and crafting effective income-generating strategies.

This is not a get-rich-quick scheme. It is a roadmap for the average person, just like you, who wants to explore the world of options and potentially build a more secure financial future.

Through my 20+ years of experience, I have learned the intricacies of options trading and discovered what works best for me. Now, I want to share that knowledge and empower you to do the same. Join me on this journey, and let us turn Fridays into potential paydays, together!

UNDERSTANDING YOUR RELATIONSHIP WITH MONEY

Have you ever wondered why some people seem to effortlessly navigate the world of finance, while others struggle? The truth is, a significant part of financial success hinges not on complex strategies or market predictions, but on something far more personal: your relationship with money.

This chapter delves into the fascinating connection between your money mindset and your options trading journey. We will explore how your beliefs, goals, and risk tolerance can significantly impact your decisions and ultimately, your results.

Lifting the Lid on Money Scripts:

We all carry invisible baggage – our money scripts. These are the unconscious beliefs and attitudes we develop about money throughout our lives, shaped by childhood experiences, societal messages, and even cultural influences.

Do any of these money scripts sound familiar?

- "I'm not good with money."
- "The rich get richer, the poor get poorer."
- "Money is the root of all evil."

These limiting beliefs can hold you back from achieving your financial goals and even sabotage your options trading success.

The good news?

You can rewrite your money script!

By identifying these negative beliefs and replacing them with empowering ones like "Money is a tool for achieving my goals" or "I can learn and grow my financial knowledge," you pave the way for a more positive and successful financial future.

Knowing Your Risk Tolerance:

Not One-Size-Fits-All!

Imagine entering a roller coaster without knowing how steep the drops are or how fast it goes. That is essentially what options trading can be like if you don't understand your risk tolerance.

Risk tolerance is your comfort level with potential financial losses. Some people are thrill-seekers, ready for the high swings of the market, while others prefer a more steady, controlled approach. Options trading offers strategies for various risk tolerances, but it is crucial to choose ones that align with yours.

Think about it this way: If you are naturally risk-averse, complex options strategies with high potential losses might not be the best fit. Identifying your risk tolerance allows you to select options strategies that suit your comfort level and potentially lead to a more sustainable and enjoyable trading experience.

Setting Your Goal:

Your Financial Roadmap!

Where do you see yourself financially? A luxurious vacation home? Early retirement? Defining your financial goals is like creating a roadmap for your options trading journey. These goals, both short-term (e.g., generating income) and long-term (e.g., retirement savings), will guide your strategy selection and help you measure your progress.

Remember, the best financial goals are SMART: Specific, Measurable, Achievable, Relevant, and Time-bound. For example, instead of a vague goal of "making more money," aim for "generating an additional $500 per month through options trading within the next 6 months." Setting clear, achievable goals keeps you motivated and focused on utilizing options trading as a tool to reach your financial aspirations.

Building a Winning Money Mindset:

Financial success is not just about numbers; it is about mindset. Developing a healthy money mindset equips you with the mental tools to navigate the options market effectively.

Here are some key aspects to consider:

- **Delayed Gratification:** The ability to resist impulsive decisions and prioritize long-term goals is crucial. Options trading is not a get-rich-quick scheme. Consistent, disciplined application of strategies is key to achieving your financial objectives.
- **Emotional Awareness:** Fear and greed are powerful emotions that can cloud judgment and lead to costly mistakes. Recognizing your emotional triggers and managing them effectively will help you make sound trading decisions based on logic, not emotions.
- **Discipline and Consistency:** Imagine training for a marathon but giving up halfway through. The same principle applies to options trading. Developing discipline and consistently applying your strategies are essential for building long-term success.

Continuous Learning:

The world of finance is dynamic, and the options market is no exception. Staying up-to-date with market trends, exploring new strategies, and continually refining your knowledge are essential for navigating the ever-changing financial landscape.

Embrace continuous learning! Read books and articles by experts, consider mentorship from experienced options traders, and utilize online resources to enhance your knowledge. Remember, the more you learn and grow, the better equipped you will be to make informed decisions and potentially thrive in the exciting world of options trading.

By understanding your relationship with money, setting clear goals, and cultivating a winning mindset, you will be well on your way to unlocking the full potential of options trading and achieving your financial dreams. So, embark on this journey of self-discovery and financial empowerment – it is a worthwhile adventure!

OPTIONS 101: Calls, Puts, Strikes, and Expiry

Welcome to the exciting world of options trading! This chapter is your foundation, introducing the key terms you will encounter throughout your options journey. We will break down concepts like calls, puts, strike prices, and expiry dates in simple, easy-to-understand language. By the end of this chapter, you will be able to confidently navigate basic options terminology and understand the core mechanics of options contracts.

Imagine the stock market as a giant playground. Stocks are like the swings and slides – they can go up and down in value. Options contracts, on the other hand, are like tickets to play on specific equipment at the playground. These tickets come with certain rules and timelines, which we will explore in detail.

Let's meet the two main players in the options world:

- **Calls:** Think of a call option as a **ticket to buy** a specific stock at a certain price by a certain time. If you believe the stock price will **go up** in the future, a call option gives you the right (but not the obligation) to purchase the stock at a predetermined price, regardless of where the market price goes. It is like having the guaranteed right to buy a swing set at a set price, even if the price of swing sets goes up in the future.

- **Puts:** A put option is the opposite side of the coin. It is like a **ticket to sell** a specific stock at a certain price by a certain time. If you believe the stock price will **go down** in the future, a put option gives you the right (but not the obligation) to sell the stock at a predetermined price, regardless of where the market price goes. Imagine having a ticket to sell your old slide at a set price, even if the price of slides goes down in the future.

Here is where things get specific:

- **Strike Price:** This is the predetermined price at which you can **buy (for calls)** or **sell (for puts)** the stock using your option contract. Think of it as the agreed-upon price for that swing set or slide, regardless of the market fluctuations.

- **Expiry Date:** This is the critical deadline by which you must exercise your option (buy or sell the stock) or the option contract expires and becomes worthless. It's like the closing time of the playground – after that, your ticket is no longer valid.

Here is an analogy to solidify these concepts:

Imagine you own a lemonade stand, and you believe the price of lemons will go up in the future. You could buy a call option for lemons at a strike price of $1 per pound. This gives you the right to buy lemons at $1 per pound, even if the market price skyrockets to $2 per pound. On the other hand, if you believe the price of lemons will crash, you could buy a put option for lemons at a strike price of $1 per pound. This gives you the right to sell lemons at $1 per pound, even if the market price drops to $0.50 per pound.

Options contracts come with a cost, called a premium, which you pay to the seller of the option. We will explore the details of premiums in later chapters.

By understanding these core terms (calls, puts, strike prices, and expiry dates), you have taken a significant step towards navigating the world of options trading. In the next chapter, we will delve deeper into the mechanics of buying and selling options contracts, using clear examples to illustrate how these concepts come to life in the market.

UNDERSTANDING THE MECHANICS OF BUYING AND SELLING OPTIONS

Now that you are familiar with the basic terminology (calls, puts, strike prices, and expiry dates) from Chapter 2, let's dive into the mechanics of options trading – buying and selling these option contracts.

Remember the playground analogy?

Think of buying an option as purchasing a ticket to play on a specific piece of equipment (the stock) for a set price (the premium) and timeframe (until expiry). Selling an option, on the other hand, is like being the one who rents out those tickets and collects the fees (premium) from the buyers.

Let's break down Buying and Selling Calls and Puts:

Buying Calls (Bullish Scenario):

You believe a stock's price will **increase** in the future (bullish).

You **buy a call option** for that stock at a specific strike price and expiry date.

You pay a premium (fee) for the call option.

If the stock price goes **above** the strike price by the expiry date, you can exercise your option to **buy** the stock at the strike price (potentially for a profit).

If the stock price stays **below** the strike price by the expiry date, the option expires worthless, and you lose only the premium you paid.

Example: Imagine you buy a call option for Apple (AAPL) with a strike price of $150 and an expiry date in 2 months. You pay a premium of $5 per share.

This means:

You have the right, but not the obligation, to buy AAPL shares at $150 per share anytime between now and the expiry date.

If AAPL goes up to $160 by expiry, you can exercise your call option and buy AAPL at $150 (a profit of $10 per share, minus the $5 premium you paid).

If AAPL stays below $150 by expiry, the option expires worthless, and you lose only the $5 premium you paid.

Buying Puts (Bearish Scenario):

You believe a stock's price will **decrease** in the future (bearish).

You **buy a put option** for that stock at a specific strike price and expiry date.

You pay a premium (fee) for the put option.

If the stock price goes **below** the strike price by the expiry date, you can exercise your option to **sell** the stock at the strike price (potentially for a profit).

If the stock price stays **above** the strike price by the expiry date, the option expires worthless, and you lose only the premium you paid.

Example: Imagine you buy a put option for Tesla (TSLA) with a strike price of $800 and an expiry date in 3 months. You pay a premium of $10 per share.

This means:

You have the right, but not the obligation, to sell TSLA shares at $800 per share anytime between now and the expiry date.

If TSLA goes down to $700 by expiry, you can exercise your put option and sell TSLA shares at $800 (a profit of $100 per share, minus the $10 premium you paid).

If TSLA stays above $800 by expiry, the option expires worthless, and you lose only the $10 premium you paid.

Selling Options (Collecting Premiums):

Selling options allows you to collect the premium (fee) from the buyer.

However, it also comes with certain risks and obligations depending on the type of option you sell (covered calls or cash-secured puts, which we will discuss in later chapters, are safer strategies for beginners).

When you sell an option, you are obligated to fulfill the buyer's contract if they choose to exercise it.

In essence, buying options gives you the right, but not the obligation, to buy or sell a stock at a certain price by a certain time. Selling options allows you to collect a premium upfront, but it also comes with the responsibility of fulfilling the contract if exercised by the buyer.

Remember, our focus in this book is on using these mechanics to potentially generate income weekly through options strategies.

Let us look at the above mechanism on a weekly basis.

Think of buying and selling options like making deals on the playground (the stock market) using your tickets (options contracts).

Buying Calls for Weekly Income:

Scenario: You believe a stock price (let us call it Company XYZ) will go up by next Friday (remember, our focus is on weekly options).

Your Ticket: You buy a call option for Company XYZ with a strike price slightly above the current market price and an expiry date next Friday.

The Deal: You pay a premium (the cost of the ticket) for the right, but not the obligation, to buy Company XYZ at the strike price by next Friday.

The Payoff: If by next Friday, Company XYZ's price rises above your strike price, you can exercise your option and buy the stock at the lower strike price, then immediately sell it at the higher market price, potentially pocketing the difference minus the premium you paid.

Example:

Let is say Company XYZ is currently trading at $20 per share.

You buy a call option with a strike price of $22 and an expiry next Friday. You pay a premium of $1 per share.

By Friday, the price of Company XYZ jumps to $25 per share.

You exercise your call option and buy 100 shares (typical options contracts deal in 100 shares) of Company XYZ at $22 per share ($22 x 100 shares = $2200).

You immediately sell those 100 shares at the current market price of $25 per share ($25 x 100 shares = $2500).

Your profit: $2500 (selling price) - $2200 (purchase price using the option) - $100 (premium) = $200 profit.

Important Note: This is a simplified example, and there's always the risk that the stock price might not go up by Friday, causing your option to expire worthless. We will discuss risk management strategies in a later chapter.

Selling Puts for Weekly Income:

Scenario: You believe the price of Company XYZ will stay relatively flat or even dip slightly by next Friday.

Your Ticket: You sell a put option for Company XYZ with a strike price slightly below the current market price and an expiry date next Friday. By selling a put option, you collect a premium upfront.

The Deal: You are essentially making a contract that obligates you to buy Company XYZ at the strike price if the owner of the put option decides to exercise it by Friday.

The Payoff: Here is the key to income generation: If the price of Company XYZ stays above the strike price by Friday, the put option expires worthless, and you keep the premium you collected upfront.

Example:

Let us say Company XYZ is again trading at $20 per share.

You sell a put option with a strike price of $18 and an expiry next Friday. You collect a premium of $1 per share.

By Friday, the price of Company XYZ stays at $20 per share.

The put option expires worthless because nobody wants to sell you the stock at a higher price ($18) when the market price is $20.

You keep the premium of $1 per share ($1 x 100 shares = $100 profit).

Remember: There is also the risk that the price of Company XYZ falls significantly by Friday. If the put option holder decides to exercise the option (because they can sell the stock to you at a higher price than the falling market price), you will be obligated to buy the stock at the strike price, potentially at a loss. We will address these risks and how to manage them in detail later.

Key Takeaways:

By buying calls for stocks you believe will go up and selling puts for stocks you believe will stay flat or slightly down, you can potentially generate weekly income through options strategies. However, it's crucial to understand the risks involved and employ proper risk management techniques, which we will explore in future chapters.

THE CLOCK IS TICKING: TIME DECAY AND OPTIONS PRICING

Imagine you have a fresh, delicious slice of chocolate cake. Over time, that cake starts to lose its magic. It dries out, the frosting loses its sparkle, and its overall appeal diminishes. In the world of options trading, there is a similar force at play, constantly working against you – **time decay**, also known as theta.

What is Time Decay (Theta)?

Time decay is the enemy of options contracts. It represents the gradual decrease in an option's value as time passes towards its expiry date. Think of it like that slice of cake – the closer you get to expiry, the less valuable the option becomes.

Why Does Time Decay Happen?

There are two main reasons why options lose value over time:

1. **Reduced Time Value:** An option contract grants you the **right, but not the obligation**, to buy (call) or sell

(put) a stock at a certain price by a certain time. The closer you get to expiry, the less time there is to exercise that right and potentially profit from a favorable price movement. As the window of opportunity shrinks, so does the option's value.

2. **Intrinsic Value vs. Time Value:** An option's price is made up of two components: intrinsic value and time value. Intrinsic value is the difference between the strike price and the current market price of the stock (if it is a call option in-the-money) or vice versa (if it is a put option in-the-money). Time value represents the potential for the stock price to move in your favor before expiry. As time decays, the time value component shrinks, dragging the overall price of the option down.

How Does Time Decay Affect Your Weekly Options Strategy?

Since our focus is on generating income through weekly options, time decay becomes a significant factor to consider.

Here is why:

- **Faster Decay:** Weekly options have a shorter lifespan compared to monthly options. This means time decay works in your favor for certain income-generating strategies. For example, if you are selling puts and the stock price stays flat, the option will expire worthless faster, allowing you to keep the premium you collected.
- **Time is Money:** Being aware of time decay allows you to choose options with expiry dates that align with your strategy. For short-term income plays, weekly options can be advantageous due to the faster erosion of time value.

Visualizing Time Decay:

Imagine a chart with two lines representing the price of a call option (blue line) and the underlying stock price (orange line) over time. The x-axis represents the time remaining until expiry, and the y-axis represents the price.

- **At the beginning (point A):** The time value is high (reflected in the premium paid for the option), as there's significant time for the stock price to move and potentially make the option profitable.
- **As time progresses (point B):** The stock price remains flat, but the call option price (blue line) starts to decline due to time decay. The time value component is diminishing.
- **As we approach expiry (point C):** The option price (blue line) continues to decay, approaching zero if the stock price remains unchanged. Time value has almost eroded completely, leaving only the intrinsic value (if any).

This is a simplified illustration. In reality, stock prices can fluctuate, impacting the option price in conjunction with time decay. However, this chart effectively highlights the concept of time decay and its erosive effect on option value, especially as expiry approaches.

Understanding time decay is crucial for profiting from options strategies. In the next chapter, we will explore another key factor impacting option prices – volatility.

THE VOLATILITY FACTOR: HOW MARKET SWINGS AFFECT OPTIONS

Imagine a teeter totter. When one child sits high on one end, the other child swings way up in the air. But when they both sit in the middle, the teeter totter barely moves. In the world of options, volatility (vega) acts like an energetic child on the teeter totter. The more volatile the market (the more the stock price swings up and down), the higher the option's price will be, and vice versa.

What is Volatility (Vega)?

Vega is a Greek letter (uppercase: B) used in options pricing to represent the sensitivity of an option's price to changes in the underlying stock's volatility. In simpler terms, vega tells you how much the price of an option will change if the market's volatility swings up or down.

A stable stock price with little movement (low volatility) makes options contracts less valuable. Why? Because the chance of the stock price making a significant move in your favor (for calls) or against you (for puts) before expiry is lower. Think of our teeter totter again – with little movement on one side (stable stock price), there is less potential for a large swing on the other side (option price).

On the other hand, a volatile market with frequent price swings (high volatility) makes options more expensive. This is because the increased volatility creates a greater chance of the stock price moving significantly before expiry, potentially leading to a bigger payoff from your options strategy. High volatility is like that energetic child on the teeter totter – it creates the potential for larger swings in the option price.

Understanding vega is crucial for profiting from weekly options strategies.

Here is why:

Capitalizing on Volatility: During periods of high volatility, you can potentially benefit by selling options (calls or puts) because the options premium will be higher due to the increased chance of price movements.

Hedging During Low Volatility: In low volatility periods, it might be better to consider alternative strategies or use options cautiously. Since option prices are lower due to the lower chance of significant price swings, selling options might not be as profitable.

Volatility: Opportunity or Risk? Understanding the Double-Edged Sword

A volatile market, with prices swinging up and down, can affect options in two key ways:

Opportunity: Increased volatility often leads to higher option prices (due to vega). This can be advantageous if you are using strategies like selling options to collect premium.

Risk: The same volatility that inflates option prices can also magnify potential losses. If the stock price swings against your position unexpectedly, you could face significant losses.

So, how do you approach volatility – as an opportunity or a risk? The answer depends on your options strategy and risk tolerance.

Volatility as an Opportunity:

Selling Options: When the market is volatile, the price of options (vega) increases. This can be a good time to consider **selling options** (calls or puts) to collect premium. Since the option price is higher due to the increased chance of price movements, you can potentially generate a larger income from the premium.

Directional Plays (Carefully): If you have a strong conviction about the direction of the stock price (up or down) during a volatile period, you could explore **buying options** (calls for uptrend, puts for downtrend). Volatility can amplify your potential profits if the stock price moves significantly in your favor. However, this strategy also carries a higher risk of substantial losses if the price goes against you.

Volatility as a Risk:

Unexpected Swings: Volatility can be unpredictable. While it can create opportunities, it can also lead to unexpected and sharp price movements against your options position. This can result in significant losses, especially if you are not using proper risk management techniques.

Lower Probability of Profit: During periods of low volatility, the chance of the stock price making a significant move in your favor (for calls) or against you (for puts) before expiry is lower. This can make it more challenging to generate profits from options strategies that rely on price movements.

Key Takeaway:

Volatility is a double-edged sword in the world of options. It can present opportunities for higher profits, but it also carries the risk of magnified losses. Understanding vega and how volatility impacts options prices is crucial for navigating both sides of this coin. In the next chapter, we will explore essential risk management techniques to help you mitigate these risks and approach options trading with more confidence.

MANAGING RISK: Stop-Loss Orders and Your Safety Net

Imagine entering a thrilling amusement park. The rides might be exhilarating, but you wouldn't jump on a rollercoaster without a safety harness, right? The same concept applies to options trading – you need a safety net to manage risk. This chapter will introduce you to essential risk management techniques, with a focus on stop-loss orders, to help you navigate the exciting world of options with more confidence.

Why is Risk Management Important?

Options trading offers the potential for significant rewards, but it also comes with inherent risks. The market can be unpredictable, and unexpected price movements can quickly erode your profits or even lead to losses. Proper risk management helps you mitigate these risks and protect your capital.

Think of risk management as your personal safety net in the options trading playground.

It helps you:

Limit Potential Losses: By setting stop-loss orders, you can define the maximum amount you are willing to lose on a particular trade. This helps prevent emotional decisions and keeps your losses controlled.

Protect Your Capital: Effective risk management safeguards your overall trading capital, allowing you to continue exploring options strategies without jeopardizing your financial stability.

Trade with Confidence: Knowing you have a risk management plan in place allows you to approach options trading with a calmer and more composed mindset.

Stop-Loss Orders: Your Basic Safety Net Tool

A stop-loss order is a basic but powerful risk management tool. It instructs your broker to automatically sell your option contract (if you bought a call or put) or close out your short option position (if you sold a call or put) when the underlying stock price reaches a specific level. This helps you limit potential losses if the market moves against your position.

Setting Stop-Loss Orders:

There are different ways to set stop-loss orders, and the specific approach will depend on your options strategy and risk tolerance.

The two common methods are:

1. Percentage-Based Stop: Set a stop-loss order that triggers when the stock price moves a certain percentage (e.g.,5% or 10%) against your desired outcome.

Example:

You buy a call option on TechCo with a strike price of $100. You believe the stock price will rise above $100 by next Friday (remember our focus is on weekly options).

Setting Your Stop-Loss:

You decide to use a 5% percentage-based stop-loss. This means you are willing to accept a maximum loss of 5% on the trade if the stock price moves against you.

Calculating the Stop-Loss Price:

A 5% loss from the current stock price (let's say it's $95) translates to $95 x (1 - 5%) = $90.25.

Placing the Order:

You instruct your broker to place a stop-loss order to sell your call option **if** the price of TechCo stock falls to $90.25 or below.

How it Works**:**

Scenario 1: Winning Trade: If by next Friday, the price of TechCo rises above $100, your call option becomes profitable, and you can choose to exercise or sell it at a higher market price.

Scenario 2: Activated Stop-Loss: If, however, the price of TechCo falls and reaches $90.25 or below before next Friday, your stop-loss order will be triggered. Your broker will automatically sell your call option, limiting your loss to around 5% (the difference between your purchase price and the stop-loss price).

Key Points about Percentage-Based Stops:

Adaptable: You can adjust the stop-loss percentage based on your risk tolerance and the volatility of the stock. For example, you might use a tighter stop-loss (lower percentage) for a more volatile stock.

Not Guaranteed: Remember, stop-loss orders are not foolproof. In a highly volatile market, the stock price might rapidly drop below your stop-loss level before the order gets filled, resulting in a slightly larger loss.

Tailor to Your Strategy: The ideal stop-loss percentage will vary depending on your specific options strategy and goals. As you gain experience, you will develop a better understanding of how to set appropriate stop-loss levels for different situations.

Percentage-based stop-loss orders are a simple yet powerful way to manage risk in options trading. By incorporating them into your strategy, you can trade with more confidence and protect your capital from unexpected market swings.

2. Price-Based Stop: Remember, a stop-loss order acts like your safety net, automatically exiting your options position when the stock price reaches a predetermined level to limit your potential losses.

Price-Based Stops in Action:

Imagine you are considering buying a call option for a stock called "Technovation Inc." (ticker symbol: TECHI) that's currently trading at $50 per share. You believe the stock price will rise in the coming week, so you are looking to profit from this potential upward movement.

Here is how a price-based stop-loss order can help you manage risk:

Define Your Acceptable Loss: Before buying the call option, decide the maximum amount of money you are willing to lose on this trade. Let's say your acceptable loss is $100.

Calculate Your Stop-Loss Price: Knowing the acceptable loss amount and the current stock price, you can calculate your stop-loss price. In this case, if you are willing to lose $100 and the stock is $50 per share, your stop-loss price would be:

Stop-Loss Price = Current Price - Acceptable Loss

Stop-Loss Price = $50 - $100

Stop-Loss Price = $40 per share

Place the Stop-Loss Order: When you buy the call option, instruct your broker to place a stop-loss sell order on the option contract. This order will automatically sell your call option if the underlying stock price (TECHI) falls to $40 per share.

Why is this important?

The market is unpredictable. While you believe the price will rise, there is always a chance it could go down.

Here is how the stop-loss order helps:

Limits Losses: If the price of TECHI unexpectedly drops below $40, your stop-loss order will get triggered, and your call option will be sold automatically. This limits your loss to the premium you paid for the option, which is typically a much smaller amount than $100 (your acceptable loss limit).

Protects Capital: By managing your risk with a stop-loss order, you prevent a potentially larger loss that could impact your overall trading capital. This allows you to stay in the game and explore other options strategies.

Remember:

- Price-based stops are not perfect. In a volatile market, the stock price might gap down quickly, briefly dipping below your stop-loss price before bouncing back. This could cause your option to be sold at a lower price than intended.
- Regularly monitor your positions and adjust stop-loss orders as needed based on market conditions and your risk tolerance.

Price-based stop-loss orders are a fundamental risk management tool for options traders. By setting a clear dollar amount you are willing to lose on a trade and translating that into a specific stop-loss price, you can take control of your risk and protect your capital. This allows you to approach options trading with more confidence and potentially navigate the ups and downs of the market more effectively.

This chapter just scratched the surface of risk management. In the following chapters, we will delve deeper into additional strategies and techniques to help you become a more confident and risk-aware weekly options trader.

THE POWER OF WEEKLY OPTIONS: Strategies for Different Markets

Regular stock options contracts typically expire monthly. However, there is a dynamic world within options trading known as **weekly options**. These contracts, as the name suggests, expire on a weekly basis, offering a unique set of advantages for traders seeking to generate income.

What are Weekly Options and Why Consider Them?

Weekly options function similarly to their monthly counterparts. You have the right, but not the obligation, to buy (call) or sell (put) a stock at a certain price by a specific expiry date. The key difference lies in the lifespan of the contract – weekly options expire every Friday, compared to the monthly cycle of traditional options.

This faster expiry schedule unlocks several potential benefits for income-generating strategies:

- **More Frequent Income Opportunities:** With expiry every week, weekly options allow you to potentially collect premiums more frequently than with monthly options. This can be particularly advantageous if you are focused on building a consistent stream of income from options trading.

- **Targeted Strategies:** The shorter lifespan of weekly options can be useful for adapting your strategy to shorter-term market movements. You can tailor your options positions to specific events or news catalysts that might impact the stock price within a week.
- **Faster Time Decay:** Remember from Chapter 4, time decay (theta) is the enemy of options contracts, gradually eroding their value as they approach expiry. Weekly options experience this time decay at a faster pace. This can be beneficial for certain income-generating strategies, such as selling options, where you want the option to expire worthless if the stock price remains relatively flat.

Focus: Income Generation Strategies

This book is dedicated to equipping you with the knowledge to utilize weekly options for income generation. Throughout the following chapters, we will delve into specific strategies that leverage the unique characteristics of weekly options to collect premiums and potentially generate consistent income. We will explore strategies suitable for different market conditions, allowing you to adapt your approach based on whether the market is trending upwards, downwards, or staying relatively flat.

So, buckle up and get ready to explore the exciting world of weekly options! With the right strategies and risk management in place, you can harness the power of these contracts to potentially generate income and navigate the ever-changing market landscape.

COVERED CALLS: Generating Income with a Stock You Already Own

Imagine you own a valuable painting hanging proudly in your living room. You appreciate its beauty, but wouldn't it be nice to earn some extra income by letting someone else admire it for a short while? Covered calls offer a similar concept in the world of options trading.

Let's dive into how this strategy works and how you can potentially generate income from stocks you already hold.

What is a Covered Call?

A covered call is an options strategy that allows you to earn income from a stock you already own (the "covered" part). It involves selling a call option contract on your existing shares. A call option grants the buyer the right, but not the obligation, to purchase your shares at a certain price (strike price) by a specific expiry date.

Mechanics of a Covered Call:

1. **Stock Ownership:** The foundation of a covered call is owning shares of the underlying stock. You wouldn't sell a call option on a stock you don't possess!
2. **Selling the Call Option:** You enter into an agreement with another trader (the call buyer) by selling a call option contract. This essentially gives the buyer the right to buy your shares at the strike price by the expiry date.
3. **Collecting the Premium:** In exchange for granting the buyer the right to purchase your shares, you receive a premium – a cash payment upfront. This premium represents the income you earn from the covered call strategy.

Potential Profits and Losses:

There are two main scenarios to consider when it comes to profits and losses in covered calls:

Scenario 1: Stock Price Stays Flat or Falls

- **Profit:** If the stock price stays flat or even falls by the expiry date, the call option will likely expire worthless. You get to keep the premium you collected as income, and you still own your original shares.
- **Loss:** Your potential loss is limited to the decrease in the stock price from your purchase price, minus the premium you received. For example, if you bought a stock at $50 and sold a covered call with a premium of $5, your maximum loss would be $45 per share (assuming the stock price falls to $0 by expiry).

Scenario 2: Stock Price Rises Above Strike Price

- **Profit:** If the stock price rises above the strike price by the expiry date, the call option becomes valuable, and the buyer will likely exercise their right to purchase your shares at the strike price. Your profit includes the premium you received initially, plus any potential gain from the difference between your purchase price and the strike price (up to the strike price).

- **Loss:** The potential loss here is the opportunity cost of missing out on further stock price appreciation if the price goes significantly higher than the strike price. However, you are still compensated by the premium you earned.

Covered Calls: Market Conditions and Considerations

Covered calls are generally considered a **neutral or bullish** strategy.

Here's why:

- **Neutral Market:** If you believe the stock price will stay relatively flat or experience a slight increase, covered calls allow you to generate income (premium) on your existing shares.
- **Bullish Market:** Even if you are moderately bullish on the stock's long-term potential, covered calls can help you earn additional income while you hold the stock. You capture some profit at the strike price if the buyer exercises the option, but you also benefit if the stock

price remains below the strike price and you keep your shares.

Covered calls are not without risks. Carefully consider these points before implementing this strategy:

- **Limited Upside Potential:** If the stock price significantly surpasses the strike price, you will miss out on those additional gains since you are obligated to sell at the strike price if the option is exercised.
- **Early Assignment Risk:** In rare cases, the option buyer might exercise the call option early (before expiry) if the stock price spikes unexpectedly. This could force you to sell your shares earlier than planned.

Examples of Covered Calls in Action

Understanding the mechanics of covered calls is crucial, but seeing them in action can solidify your grasp of this income-generating strategy.

Let's explore two real-world examples:

Example 1: Generating Income on a Flat Stock

Imagine you own 100 shares of a tech company, ABC Corp. (ticker symbol: ABC), that has been trading around $40 per share for the past few weeks. You believe the stock price might stay flat or experience a slight increase in the coming week.

- **Covered Call Action:** You decide to sell a covered call on your 100 shares of ABC with a strike price of $45 and an expiry date one week from now. The premium for this option is $2 per share.
- **Potential Outcomes:**
    - **Scenario 1: Flat or Downward Price Movement:** If the stock price remains around $40 or even dips slightly by expiry, the call option will likely expire worthless. Here is the breakdown:
        - Profit: You keep the premium of $2 x 100 shares = $200.
        - You still own your 100 shares of ABC stock.

- **Scenario 2: Stock Price Rises Above $45:** If the stock price unexpectedly surges above $45 by expiry, the call buyer will likely exercise their option to purchase your shares at $45 per share. Here is the outcome:
    - Profit: You receive the premium of $200 (as in scenario 1) + profit from the sale of your shares at $45 (strike price) minus your original purchase price (let's say you bought at $40). This translates to a profit of $200 + ($45 - $40) x 100 shares = $700.
    - You no longer own the 100 shares of ABC stock.

NOTE: In this example, even if the stock price stays flat, you earn income from the premium. If the price increases slightly, you still benefit. However, if the stock price shoots up significantly, you miss out on those additional gains but are still compensated for the covered call.

Example 2: Income Generation with a Bullish Bias

Let's say you own 200 shares of a retail company, XYZ Inc. (ticker symbol: XYZ), currently trading at $60 per share. You have a moderately bullish outlook on XYZ, believing it has the potential to reach $70 in the next few months.

- **Covered Call Action:** You decide to sell a covered call on your 200 shares of XYZ with a strike price of $70 and an expiry date 6 weeks from now. The premium for this option is $3 per share.
- **Potential Outcomes:**
    - **Scenario 1: Stock Price Stays Flat or Falls Below $70:** If the stock price remains around $60 or even dips slightly over the next 6 weeks, the call option will likely expire worthless. Here is the breakdown:
        - Profit: You keep the premium of $3 x 200 shares = $600.
        - You still own your 200 shares of XYZ stock.

- **Scenario 2: Stock Price Rises Above $70 by Expiry:** If the price climbs above $70 by expiry, the call buyer will likely exercise the option to purchase your shares. Here is the outcome:
    - Profit: You receive the premium of $600 (as in scenario 1) + profit from the sale of your shares at $70 (strike price) minus your original purchase price (let's say you bought at $55). This translates to a profit of $600 + ($70 - $55) x 200 shares = $2,600.
    - You no longer own the 200 shares of XYZ stock.
- **Scenario 3: Stock Price Significantly Surpasses $70:** This is where the opportunity cost comes into play. If the stock price explodes to $80 or higher, you miss out on those additional gains since you are obligated to sell at $70 if the option is exercised.

NOTE: This example highlights how covered calls can generate income even with a bullish outlook. You benefit if the price stays flat or increases moderately, but you are capped on potential profits if the stock price surges significantly.

Remember: These are simplified examples. Real-world scenarios will involve additional factors like volatility and choosing appropriate strike prices and expiry dates based on your strategy and risk tolerance. However, they effectively demonstrate how covered calls can be used to generate income from stocks while offering some protection against a potential price decline. By carefully considering the strike price, expiry date, and your overall outlook on the stock, covered calls can become a valuable tool in your options trading arsenal.

Beyond the Examples: Tailoring Covered Calls to Your Needs

The beauty of covered calls lies in their adaptability. You can customize this strategy based on your risk tolerance and market expectations:

- **Conservative Approach:** For a more conservative approach, choose a lower strike price closer to the current stock price. This reduces your premium income but also minimizes potential losses if the stock price falls. The option will be more likely to expire worthless, allowing you to keep your shares.
- **Moderately Bullish Approach:** If you are moderately bullish on the stock, consider a strike price slightly above the current price. This allows you to collect a higher premium while still capturing some potential profit if the stock price rises and the option is exercised.
- **Focus on Premium:** If your primary goal is income generation, you can choose a strike price even further above the current price to maximize the premium you receive. However, be aware that you are more likely to be assigned (forced to sell your shares) if the stock price rises significantly.

Remember: Covered calls are not a risk-free strategy. Always factor in potential early assignment and opportunity costs before implementing them.

Covered calls allow you to generate income by selling options contracts while owning the underlying stock. The next chapter will introduce you to cash-secured puts, another income-generating strategy that works on the opposite side of the equation. We will explore how you can earn income by potentially being assigned shares of a stock you are interested in owning at a favorable price.

CASH-SECURED PUTS: Earning Income by Taking on an Obligation

"Cash-secured puts allow you to collect income upfront while strategically positioning yourself for potential stock ownership at a discount. It's a great way to generate income during neutral or bearish markets, but remember, the obligation to buy the stock is the key consideration." - **Todd Harrison, Founder & CEO of Contrarian Options Trading**

Imagine you are at a store browsing the latest gadgets. You see a new phone you kind of like, but you are not sure if you want to buy it right away. Cash-secured puts offer a similar concept in the world of options trading, allowing you to earn income while keeping an "open door" to potentially owning a stock in the future.

Mechanics of Cash-Secured Puts:

1. **Setting the Stage:** You have an interest in a particular stock (let's call it "TechTron Inc.", ticker symbol: TTI) but are unsure if the price is right at this moment.

2. **Selling a Put Option:** Instead of buying the stock outright, you enter into an agreement with another trader by selling a **put option** on TTI shares. A put option grants the buyer (the other trader) the right, but

not the obligation, to **sell** their TTI shares to you at a certain price (strike price) by a specific expiry date.

3. **Securing Your Cash:** Here is the twist that makes it "cash-secured." To ensure you have the funds to potentially buy the stock if assigned (forced to buy), you need to deposit a certain amount of cash (usually equal to the strike price multiplied by the number of shares) with your broker. This cash acts as collateral, similar to a security deposit.

4. **Collecting the Premium:** In exchange for taking on the obligation to buy the stock at the strike price if assigned, you receive a premium upfront – a cash payment from the put buyer.

Potential Profits and Losses:

There are two main scenarios to consider:

Scenario 1: Stock Price Stays Flat or Rises Above Strike Price

- **Profit:** If the stock price stays flat or even rises above the strike price by expiry, the put option you sold is unlikely to be exercised by the buyer. Here is the breakdown:

- You keep the premium you received as income.
- You **don't** have to buy any shares – your cash collateral is returned by your broker.

• **Loss:** Your potential loss in this scenario is limited to the time decay (theta) of the option premium. Remember from Chapter 4, options lose value over time as they approach expiry. This loss is usually much smaller than the premium you received.

Scenario 2: Stock Price Falls Below Strike Price

• **Profit:** If the stock price falls below the strike price by expiry, the put option becomes valuable, and the buyer might exercise their right to sell their TTI shares to you at the strike price. Here is the outcome:
  - You are **assigned** (forced) to buy the shares at the strike price using your deposited cash collateral.
  - You **potentially profit** from the difference between the strike price you paid and a lower

future price, if the stock continues to decline. However, there is no guarantee the price will fall further.

- **Loss:** Your potential loss is if the stock price plummets significantly after you are assigned. However, the cash you secured beforehand limits your downside compared to simply buying the stock outright.

Risk Considerations:

- **Assignment Risk:** The biggest risk with cash-secured puts is the possibility of being assigned the stock, even if you don't necessarily want to buy it at that moment. This could happen if the stock price drops significantly.
- **Blocked Capital:** The cash you set aside as collateral is tied up until the option expires. This means you cannot use it for other investments during that period.
- **Limited Upside Potential:** If the stock price surges significantly above the strike price, you miss out on

those additional gains since you are obligated to buy at the strike price if assigned.

Overall, cash-secured puts are a strategy for income generation suitable for neutral or bearish markets. They allow you to earn a premium while potentially acquiring a stock at a discount if the price falls. However, carefully consider the risk of assignment and potential limitations before implementing this strategy.

When are Cash-Secured Puts Most Suitable?

Cash-secured puts can be a valuable tool for options traders, but understanding the appropriate market conditions is crucial.

Let us delve into why cash-secured puts are generally considered a good fit for neutral or bearish markets:

Neutral Market:

- **Scenario:** Imagine a stagnant market where stock prices are expected to remain relatively flat in the near future.

- **Cash-Secured Puts Strategy:** If you are neutral on a particular stock's outlook but interested in earning some income, cash-secured puts can be a good option. By selling a put option, you collect a premium regardless of whether the stock price stays flat or even rises slightly by expiry. There is a good chance the option won't be exercised, and you keep the premium as income.
- **Advantage:** Cash-secured puts allow you to generate income in a market where significant stock price appreciation might not be expected.

Bearish Market:

- **Scenario:** A bearish market is characterized by a general decline in stock prices.
- **Cash-Secured Puts Strategy:** If you anticipate a stock's price to fall, cash-secured puts can offer a way to potentially profit from a downturn while also potentially acquiring the stock at a discount. Here is why:

- **Profit Potential:** If the stock price falls below the strike price by expiry, the put option you sold will likely be exercised, and you will be assigned to buy the shares at the strike price. This could be lower than the current market price, allowing you to potentially buy at a discount.
- **Downside Protection:** The cash you set aside as collateral limits your potential losses compared to simply buying the stock outright. If the stock price plummets significantly, your loss is capped at the difference between the strike price and the initial cash deposit.
- **Advantage:** Cash-Secured puts allow you to potentially profit from a declining market while also positioning yourself to buy the stock at a potentially lower price.

Why Not Bullish Markets?

Cash-secured puts might not be the most optimal strategy for bullish markets where stock prices are expected to rise significantly.

Here is why:

- **Limited Upside:** If the stock price surges above the strike price, you will miss out on those additional gains since you are obligated to buy at the strike price if assigned. You will only capture the premium income and the difference between the strike price and the initial stock price (if assigned).

Alternative Strategies for Bullish Markets:

- **Bull Calls:** If you are bullish on a stock, consider buying call options instead. This allows you to profit if the stock price rises but limits your potential loss to the premium paid for the call option.

Cash-secured puts are a strategic option for income generation in neutral or bearish markets. By understanding the market conditions and potential limitations, you can effectively utilize this strategy to potentially earn income and position yourself for potential stock ownership at a discount.

Examples of Cash-Secured Puts in Action

Understanding the mechanics and suitability of cash-secured puts is essential, but seeing them in action can solidify your grasp of this strategy.

Let's explore two real-world examples:

Example 1: Generating Income on a Flat Stock

Imagine you believe shares of a retail company, "Daily Deals Inc." (ticker symbol: DDI), will likely trade sideways in the coming weeks. You are interested in potentially owning DDI stock but are content to wait for a better entry point.

- **Cash-Secured Put Action:** You decide to sell a cash-secured put on 100 shares of DDI with a strike price of $40 and an expiry date 6 weeks from now. The premium for this option is $2 per share.
- **Potential Outcomes:**
    - **Scenario 1: Flat or Upward Price Movement:** If the stock price stays around $40 or even climbs

slightly by expiry, the put option likely won't be exercised. Here is the breakdown:

- **Profit:** You keep the premium of $2 x 100 shares = $200.
- You retain the cash you deposited as collateral (usually $4,000 in this case, which is the strike price x number of shares).
- You **don't** own any DDI shares yet.

○ **Scenario 2: Stock Price Falls Below $40:** If the price dips below $40 by expiry, the put buyer might exercise their right to sell you the shares at $40. Here is the outcome:

- You are **assigned** to buy 100 shares of DDI at $40 per share, using your deposited cash collateral.
- Your potential profit depends on the future stock price. If it rebounds above $40, you could sell your shares at a profit. However, there is no guarantee of this.

This example shows how cash-secured puts can generate income (the premium) even if the stock price stays flat or rises slightly. You only acquire the stock if the price falls below your chosen strike price.

Example 2: Income and Potential Acquisition in a Bearish Market

Imagine you believe a tech company, "Cloud Nine Inc." (ticker symbol: CNI), is overvalued and its stock price is likely to decline in the coming months. You are open to owning CNI shares at a discount but want to limit your downside risk.

- **Cash-Secured Put Action:** You decide to sell a cash-secured put on 200 shares of CNI with a strike price of $60 and an expiry date 3 months from now. The premium for this option is $1.50 per share.
- **Potential Outcomes:**
    - **Scenario 1: Stock Price Stays Flat or Rises Above $60:** Similar to the first example, if the price stays flat or increases by expiry, the put option likely won't be exercised. You keep the

premium ($300) and your deposited cash collateral.

- **Scenario 2: Stock Price Falls Below $60:** If the price dips below $60 by expiry, the put buyer might exercise the option to sell you the shares. Here is the outcome:
  - You are assigned to buy 200 shares of CNI at $60 per share, using your deposited cash collateral.
  - If the stock price continues to decline, you potentially profit from the difference between your $60 strike price and the lower market price. However, there is always the risk the price could fall further.

This example highlights how cash-secured puts can be used in a bearish market to potentially profit from a falling stock price while also acquiring shares at a potentially favorable price if assigned.

Conclusion

Cash-secured puts offer a unique strategy for income generation in options trading. By carefully considering market conditions, strike prices, and potential risks, you can leverage this strategy to earn premiums and potentially position yourself for stock ownership at a discount. Remember, it's crucial to understand the mechanics, potential profits and losses, and risk considerations before implementing cash-secured puts in your investment strategy.

Quote by Karen Abraham, Options Strategist at E*Trade:

"Cash-secured puts are a fantastic strategy for income-oriented investors who are comfortable potentially owning a particular stock. By taking on the obligation to buy at a specific price, you can earn income upfront while potentially acquiring shares at a favorable price."

BEYOND BASICS: Exploring Additional Weekly Strategies

While covered calls and cash-secured puts are powerful income-generating tools, the world of options strategies extends far beyond these fundamentals. This chapter will briefly introduce a few **additional strategies that can potentially yield income**, but it is important to understand they involve greater complexity and risk.

Here is a taste of what awaits you as you delve deeper into options:

- **Bull Put Spreads:** This strategy combines buying a put option and selling a call option with different strike prices on the same underlying stock. It allows you to profit if the stock price stays flat or rises but limits your potential gains.
- **Bear Call Spreads:** This strategy involves selling a call option and buying a call option with a higher strike price on the same underlying stock. It allows you to profit if the stock price falls but limits your potential

profit and increases your risk compared to a cash-secured put.

- **Butterfly Spreads:** These involve a combination of buying and selling multiple options contracts with different strike prices on the same underlying stock. Butterfly spreads can be designed for various outcomes, such as profiting from a limited price movement in the stock.

- **Straddles and Strangles:** Straddles involve buying both a put and a call option with the same strike price, while strangles involve buying options with different strike prices. These strategies profit from significant price movements in the underlying stock, either up or down, but require a larger upfront investment and carry substantial risk.

Mechanics and the Risk/Reward Trade-Off

The additional income-generating strategies mentioned above involve more intricate structures compared to covered calls and cash-secured puts.

Let's explore the mechanics of each and highlight the increased complexity and risk:

- **Bull Put Spreads:**
  - **Mechanics:** You buy a put option (providing downside protection) at a lower strike price and simultaneously sell a call option (limiting potential gains) at a higher strike price on the same stock. You profit if the stock stays flat or rises by expiry, but your gains are capped by the difference in strike prices minus the premiums paid/received.
  - **Complexity and Risk:** While this strategy offers some downside protection, it requires monitoring two options and understanding how their Greeks (measures of option sensitivity) interact. There is also the risk of the stock price moving significantly outside your chosen strike prices, resulting in potential losses.
- **Bear Call Spreads:**
  - **Mechanics:** You sell a call option (generating income) at a lower strike price and

simultaneously buy a call option (limiting your profit potential) at a higher strike price on the same stock. You profit if the stock price falls by expiry, but your gains are capped and you take on more risk than a cash-secured put because you are not obligated to buy the stock.

- **Complexity and Risk:** Similar to bull put spreads, this strategy involves managing two options and understanding their Greeks. There is also the risk of the stock price not falling as much as anticipated, resulting in missed gains, or even rising significantly, leading to potential losses if the sold call option is exercised.

- **Butterfly Spreads:**
  - **Mechanics:** These involve buying and selling multiple options contracts with various strike prices on the same stock. Different butterfly spread structures exist, but they generally aim to profit from limited price movement in the underlying stock.

- **Complexity and Risk:** Butterfly spreads involve managing several options contracts simultaneously, making them more complex than single options strategies. Misunderstanding the Greeks and their interactions can lead to substantial losses.

- **Straddles and Strangles:**
  - **Mechanics:** Straddles involve buying both a put and a call option with the same strike price, while strangles involve buying options with different strike prices (one put, one call). These strategies profit from significant price movements, either up or down, by expiry.
  - **Complexity and Risk:** Straddles and strangles require a significant upfront investment as you are buying multiple options contracts. They are high-risk strategies because if the stock price doesn't move much, you lose a substantial amount on the premiums paid.

Detailed Explanations of the Above Strategies:

Bull Put Spread

A bull put spread is an options strategy designed to profit from a **limited upside move or neutral movement** in the price of the underlying stock. It combines buying a put option with a lower strike price and selling a put option with a higher strike price on the same underlying asset and with the same expiration date.

Here is an example to illustrate how a bull put spread works:

Scenario:

- You are bullish or neutral on the stock price of XYZ Company (XYZ).
- The current stock price of XYZ is $50.

Implementation:

1. **Buy a put option with a strike price of $45 (Lower Strike):** This gives you the right, but not the obligation, to buy 100 shares of XYZ at $45 per share by the expiry date. This purchase protects you if the stock price falls significantly.

2. **Sell a put option with a strike price of $55 (Higher Strike):** This obligates you to buy 100 shares of XYZ at $55 per share if the put option is exercised by the expiry date (usually by another trader). You will collect a premium for selling this put option.

Profit Potential:

- Your maximum profit in this scenario is limited to the difference between the premiums received from selling the higher strike put option and the premium paid for buying the lower strike put option.
- You will also profit if the stock price rises modestly by expiry, as long as it remains above your lower strike price (where you have the right to buy at a discount).

Risk and Considerations:

- Your maximum loss is limited to the premium paid for buying the lower strike put option. This defines the potential downside risk of the strategy.
- You will lose money if the stock price falls significantly below your lower strike price by expiry. In this case,

your put option will be exercised, and you will be obligated to buy the stock at the higher strike price, potentially at a loss.

Benefits of Bull Put Spread:

- Defined risk: Limited potential loss compared to buying a naked put option.
- Profits from limited upside or neutral movement: Can profit even if the stock price doesn't rise significantly, as long as it stays above your lower strike price.
- Income generation: Collects premium from selling the higher strike put option.

Who Might Use a Bull Put Spread?

- Investors who are bullish or neutral on a stock but want to limit their downside risk.
- Investors who want to generate income through options premiums while remaining somewhat optimistic about the stock price.

This is a simplified example, and real-world options trading involves various factors like time decay, volatility, and transaction costs. It is crucial to understand these factors and practice paper trading before risking real capital.

Bear Call Spread

Imagine you are bearish on a stock (ABC) and believe its price will decline in the near future. However, you are uncertain about the exact extent of the decline. You want to profit from a potential price drop while limiting your risk and potential losses.

Strategy: Bear Call Spread

Steps:

1. **Sell an Out-of-the-Money Call Option:** You sell a call option on ABC with a strike price **higher** than the current market price. This generates immediate premium income but obligates you to sell the underlying stock (ABC) at the strike price if the option is exercised by the buyer.
2. **Buy a Higher Out-of-the-Money Call Option:** You simultaneously buy a call option on ABC with an even

higher strike price than the one you sold. This additional call option provides you with the right, but not the obligation, to buy the stock at the higher strike price if the stock price unexpectedly rises.

Profit Potential:

Your maximum profit in this scenario is limited to the premium income you receive when you sell the first (lower strike price) call option, minus the premium you pay when you buy the second (higher strike price) call option.

Risk and Limitation:

- **Limited Profit Potential:** Compared to a naked put option (selling a put option without buying any additional options), a bear call spread limits your potential profit.
- **Potential Loss:** If the stock price unexpectedly rises significantly and surpasses both strike prices by the expiry date, you could be assigned (forced to buy) the stock at the lower strike price you sold and then be obligated to exercise your higher strike price call

option to buy the stock at a potentially even higher price. This results in a loss.

Benefits:

- **Defined Risk:** The maximum loss in a bear call spread is limited to the difference between the two strike prices minus the premium income received.
- **Income Generation:** You earn premium income upfront from selling the lower strike price call option.

Who Might Use a Bear Call Spread?

- Investors who are bearish on a stock but want to limit their downside risk.
- Investors who want to generate income while remaining bearish on a stock's price movement.

This is a simplified example. Before using a bear call spread or any options strategy, ensure you thoroughly understand the risks involved and align the strategy with your overall investment goals and risk tolerance.

Butterfly Spread

Let's say you are cautiously optimistic about the future of Stock XYZ. You believe the price might stay somewhat stable or experience a limited move in either direction. Here is how you could potentially use a butterfly spread to capitalize on this scenario:

The Scenario:

- Current Stock Price (XYZ): $50

The Butterfly Spread:

- **Buy 1 Call Option (Lower Strike Price):** Strike Price $45 (slightly in-the-money)
- **Sell 2 Call Options (Middle Strike Price):** Strike Price $50 (at-the-money)
- **Buy 1 Call Option (Higher Strike Price):** Strike Price $55 (slightly out-of-the-money)

Explanation:

- By buying a call option with a lower strike price ($45), you profit if the stock price rises significantly above

$45 by expiry. However, this profit is capped because you also sold two calls at the $50 strike price.

- Selling the two calls at the $50 strike price generates premium income and acts as the "center" of the butterfly. You ideally want the stock price to stay near $50 by expiry to maximize this premium income.
- Buying a call option with a higher strike price ($55) offers some protection against a substantial price increase but limits your overall potential gains.

Profit Potential:

- Your maximum profit is limited to the difference between the premium received from selling the two middle calls and the premiums paid for the two outer calls. This profit is achieved if the stock price stays near the $50 strike price by expiry.

Risk and Considerations:

- Your maximum loss is limited to the premiums paid for all three call options. This loss occurs if the stock

price moves significantly outside the range of your chosen strike prices by expiry.
- Butterfly spreads are complex strategies and require careful monitoring. Unexpected market movements or changes in volatility can impact the profitability of the spread.

This is a simplified example. Before implementing a butterfly spread, conduct thorough research, understand the risks involved, and consider your risk tolerance and overall trading goals.

Straddle vs. Strangle

Let's say you are interested in Apple (AAPL) stock but are unsure if the price will go up or down significantly in the next week. You could use options strategies to potentially profit from a large price movement in either direction. Here is an example comparing a Straddle and a Strangle using AAPL weekly options:

Scenario: AAPL stock price is currently at $150.

Straddle:

- You buy one AAPL weekly call option with a strike price of $150 (at-the-money) and one AAPL weekly put option with a strike price of $150 (at-the-money).
- **Cost:** The combined cost will be the premium paid for both the call and put option. Let's assume the call option premium is $5 and the put option premium is $4, for a total cost of $9 per share.
- **Potential Profit:** This strategy profits if the stock price moves significantly up or down from $150 by expiry.
    - **Stock Price Increases:** If AAPL goes up to $160 by expiry, you could exercise your call option for a $10 per share profit (minus the $9 premium paid).
    - **Stock Price Decreases:** If AAPL goes down to $140 by expiry, you could exercise your put option for a $10 per share profit (minus the $9 premium paid).
- **Potential Loss:** This strategy suffers a loss if the stock price stays relatively flat near $150 by expiry. In this case, both the call and put option expire

worthless, and you lose the entire premium paid ($9 per share).

Strangle:

- You buy one AAPL weekly call option with a strike price of $160 (out-of-the-money) and one AAPL weekly put option with a strike price of $140 (out-of-the-money).
- **Cost:** The combined cost will be lower than the straddle because the options are further away from the current stock price. Let's assume the call option premium is $3 and the put option premium is $2, for a total cost of $5 per share.
- **Potential Profit:** This strategy profits if the stock price makes a significant move up above $160 or down below $140 by expiry.
    - **Stock Price Increases:** Similar to the straddle, you would profit if AAPL goes up to $160 by expiry, exercising the call option for a profit (minus the premium paid). However, the profit potential is smaller compared to the straddle

because the call option was purchased at a lower strike price.

- **Stock Price Decreases:** Similar to the straddle, you would profit if AAPL goes down to $140 by expiry, exercising the put option for a profit (minus the premium paid). Again, the profit potential is smaller compared to the straddle.

• **Potential Loss:** This strategy suffers a loss if the stock price stays relatively flat near $150 by expiry, similar to the straddle. However, the potential loss is lower compared to the straddle because the option premiums were cheaper.

Key Differences:

• **Cost:** Straddle has a higher upfront cost due to at-the-money options.
• **Profit Potential:** Straddle offers potentially higher profits for larger price movements but also has a higher chance of expiring worthless.

- **Break-Even Point:** Straddle requires a larger price movement (up or down) to become profitable compared to the strangle.

Choosing Between Straddle and Strangle:

The choice between a straddle and a strangle depends on your conviction about the stock price movement and your risk tolerance.

- **Straddle:** Choose a straddle if you have a strong feeling the stock price will move significantly in either direction and are willing to pay a higher upfront cost for potentially larger profits.
- **Strangle:** Choose a strangle if you believe the stock price will move but are unsure of the direction. It offers a lower-cost entry point and the potential to profit from larger price movements while limiting your risk compared to a straddle.

Remember: Straddles and strangles are complex strategies with high upfront costs and a significant risk of losing the entire premium paid if the stock price movement is minimal. It is crucial to understand the risks involved and use them only with proper risk management techniques like position sizing and stop-loss orders.

While these additional strategies offer the potential for higher income, they come with increased complexity and risk. It is crucial to understand the mechanics, risk factors, and how the Greeks impact these strategies before implementing them.

Before You Dive into the Deep End: Master the Basics First

The world of options offers a vast array of strategies, many with enticing income-generating potential. However, as you have seen in this chapter, venturing beyond fundamental strategies like covered calls and cash-secured puts introduces significant complexity and risk.

Think of these additional strategies like advanced culinary techniques. While a master chef can create intricate dishes with multiple components, a home cook needs to solidify their foundation by mastering basic skills like sauteing and baking. Similarly, in options trading, mastering core strategies like covered calls and cash-secured puts equips you with a solid foundation before attempting more complex maneuvers.

Here is why focusing on the basics first is wise:

Solid Foundation: Understanding core strategies builds a strong foundation for comprehending more intricate ones later.

Risk Management: Mastering basic strategies allows you to manage risk effectively before tackling options with more complex risk profiles.

Confidence Building: Success with fundamental strategies builds confidence and a deeper understanding of options mechanics before venturing into uncharted territory.

Remember, the options market offers a spectrum of opportunities. While the allure of higher income from complex strategies is understandable, prioritize mastering the basics first. This will equip you with the knowledge and experience to navigate the options world with greater confidence and potentially achieve your financial goals.

RISK MANAGEMENT DEEP DIVE: Beyond Stop-Loss Orders

Stop-loss orders are a valuable tool, but options trading requires a more comprehensive risk management toolbox. Here, we will delve into advanced techniques to help you navigate the options market with greater confidence:

1. Understanding the Greeks:

The Greeks are a set of letters representing key metrics that measure the sensitivity of an option's price to various factors. While they may seem complex, a basic understanding of a few key Greeks can significantly improve your risk management.

- **Delta (Δ):** Imagine Delta as a measure of how much the option's price will change (move) for every $1 change in the underlying stock price.
    - A Delta of 0.5 indicates the option's price will likely move 50 cents for every $1 move in the stock price.

- A Delta closer to 1 (or -1 for put options) suggests the option's price will move almost in line with the stock price.
- **Gamma (Γ):** Gamma reflects how quickly the Delta itself changes. Think of it like the acceleration of the option's price movement.
  - A high Gamma indicates the Delta will change rapidly as the stock price moves, potentially leading to faster profits or losses.
  - A low Gamma suggests a more gradual change in Delta, offering a potentially more stable scenario.
- **Rho (P):** Rho measures how sensitive an option's price is to changes in interest rates.
  - This is generally less relevant for short-term (weekly) options strategies we have focused on, but understanding its existence is important for well-rounded risk management.

2. Portfolio Diversification:

Don't put all your eggs in one basket! Diversification is a cornerstone of risk management in any investment strategy, and options trading is no exception.

Here is how diversification applies:

Underlying Assets: Spread your options trades across different stocks or sectors to avoid being overly exposed to a single company's performance.

Options Strategies: Don't rely solely on one options strategy. Consider incorporating a mix of covered calls, cash-secured puts, or even bull/bear spreads to balance your risk profile.

Expiry Dates: Stagger your option expiry dates to avoid having all your positions expiring at once. This helps spread out potential gains and losses and reduces vulnerability to short-term market fluctuations.

3. Position Sizing:

Position sizing refers to the amount of capital you allocate to each options trade. This plays a crucial role in managing risk:

Risk Tolerance: Align your position size with your risk tolerance. If you are a conservative investor, allocate a smaller percentage of your capital per trade.

Maximum Loss Potential: Before entering a trade, determine the maximum potential loss you are comfortable with for that specific position. Never risk more than you can afford to lose.

Account Size: Consider your overall account size when allocating capital. A larger account allows for potentially larger positions while maintaining a similar risk profile compared to a smaller account.

By incorporating these advanced risk management techniques alongside stop-loss orders, you can develop a more comprehensive approach to options trading. Remember, understanding the Greeks, practicing portfolio diversification, and implementing strategic position sizing will equip you to navigate the options market with greater control and potentially achieve your financial goals.

TECHNICAL ANALYSIS FOR OPTIONS TRADERS:
Identifying Opportunities

While understanding options strategies is crucial, pinpointing potential entry and exit points is essential for successful options trading. This chapter delves into how basic technical analysis indicators can illuminate trading opportunities for your weekly options strategies.

Technical analysis involves studying historical price charts and market data to identify trends, potential support and resistance levels, and trading signals. It is a valuable tool, but remember, it is not a foolproof prediction method. Technical indicators should be used in conjunction with other factors like fundamental analysis and your overall options strategy.

Here are a few key technical analysis indicators well-suited for identifying potential opportunities for your weekly options trades:

1. **Moving Averages (MA):**

    - **Concept:** Moving averages smooth out price fluctuations by averaging a stock's price over a specific period (e.g.,50-day, 200-day moving average).

    - **How it Helps with Weekly Options:**
        - **Upward Sloping Moving Average:** A consistently rising moving average can indicate an uptrend,potentially suggesting opportunities for **bull call options** (where you profit if the stock price rises).
        - **Downtrending Moving Average:** A consistently falling moving average can indicate a downtrend,potentially suggesting opportunities for **bear put options** (where you profit if the stock price falls).

2. **Relative Strength Index (RSI):**

    - **Concept:** The RSI measures a stock's recent price movements to gauge whether it's oversold (below 30) or overbought (above 70).

- **How it Helps with Weekly Options:**
  - **Oversold RSI (below 30):** An oversold RSI might suggest the stock price is due for a rebound, potentially signifying an opportunity for **bull call options**.
  - **Overbought RSI (above 70):** An overbought RSI might suggest the stock price is inflated and could experience a correction, potentially signifying an opportunity for **bear put options**.

3. Bollinger Bands (BB):

- **Concept:** Bollinger Bands consist of an upper and lower band around a moving average. The bands expand and contract based on the stock's price volatility.
- **How it Helps with Weekly Options:**
  - **Narrowing Bollinger Bands:** Narrowing bands might indicate a period of low volatility, potentially a good time to enter a **neutral options strategy** (like a covered call) that benefits from stable stock prices.

- **Expanding Bollinger Bands:** Expanding bands might indicate a period of increased volatility, potentially a good time for **debit spreads** (where you pay more upfront but have a defined risk and profit potential).

4. **Support and Resistance Levels:**

- **Concept:** Support levels are price areas where the stock price tends to find buying interest and bounce back up. Conversely, resistance levels are areas where the stock price tends to face selling pressure and may be rejected.
- **How it Helps with Weekly Options:**
    - **Breakout Above Resistance:** A breakout above a resistance level might indicate a potential uptrend, suggesting opportunities for **bull call options**.
    - **Breakdown Below Support:** A breakdown below a support level might indicate a potential downtrend, suggesting opportunities for **bear put options**.

Important Considerations:

- **Confirmation:** Don't rely solely on one indicator. Look for confirmation signals from other indicators or price action before entering a trade.
- **False Signals:** Technical indicators can generate false signals. Combine them with your understanding of the options strategy and the underlying stock.
- **Options Expiration:** Remember, you are dealing with weekly options. Choose indicators with timeframes relevant to your expiry dates (e.g., shorter-term moving averages like 10-day or 20-day MA).

Beyond the Indicators

Technical analysis indicators are powerful tools, but they shouldn't be the sole factor in your options trading decisions. Here are some additional considerations:

- **Fundamental Analysis:** Understand the company's financial health, industry trends, and overall market sentiment before entering a trade.

- **Options Strategy Selection:** Choose an options strategy that aligns with your market outlook and risk tolerance.
- **Risk Management:** Always implement proper risk management techniques like position sizing and stop-loss orders.

By combining technical analysis with a well-rounded understanding of options strategies, fundamental analysis, and sound risk management, you can develop a more comprehensive approach to identifying trading opportunities and potentially achieving your financial goals in the options market.

Technical analysis is a skill that takes time and practice to master. Start by familiarizing yourself with the basic indicators mentioned above, experiment with paper trading (simulated trading), and gradually build your confidence before risking real capital.

THE LONG GAME: Recap, Realistic Expectations, and Moving Forward

You have reached the final chapter of this options trading guide. Throughout this journey, we have explored the exciting world of options, delving into core strategies, risk management techniques, and even a glimpse into technical analysis.

Now, let's recap the key takeaways, set some realistic expectations, and discuss how to keep moving forward on your options trading path.

A Foundation for Options Success

We began by demystifying options contracts, understanding the basic mechanics of calls and puts. We then delved into powerful income-generating strategies like covered calls and cash-secured puts, equipping you with tools to potentially earn consistent returns. The importance of risk management was woven throughout, emphasizing techniques like stop-loss orders and position sizing to navigate the market with greater control.

As we ventured further, we explored additional options strategies, delving into the world of spreads and understanding the increased complexity and risk involved. We also dipped our toes into technical analysis, learning how basic indicators can potentially help identify trading opportunities for your weekly options strategies.

Setting Realistic Expectations

The options market offers a vast array of possibilities, but it is crucial to maintain realistic expectations.

Here is what to keep in mind:

- **Options are Powerful, But Not a Magic Formula:** Options can be a valuable tool, but they don't guarantee riches. Consistent success requires discipline, sound strategy selection, and a healthy dose of patience.
- **Learning Curve and Experience Matter:** Don't expect to become an options whiz overnight. Mastering options takes time, dedication, and

experience. Embrace the learning process, and prioritize paper trading before risking real capital.

- **Losses are Inevitable:** Even the most seasoned options traders experience losses. The key is to manage risk effectively, learn from mistakes, and adjust your approach as needed. Focus on becoming a well-rounded options trader, not just a winning one.

Risk Management

Risk management is not an afterthought; it is the cornerstone of successful options trading.

Here are some key takeaways to remember:

- **Start Small:** Begin with smaller positions as you build your confidence and experience.
- **Stop-Loss Orders:** Utilize stop-loss orders to limit potential losses on your trades.
- **Position Sizing:** Allocate a reasonable portion of your capital to each trade, considering your risk tolerance and overall account size.

- **Diversification:** Spread your options trades across different assets and strategies to avoid overexposure to a single stock or market movement.

The Importance of Ongoing Learning

The options market is dynamic and constantly evolving. Here is how to stay ahead of the curve:

- **Stay Informed:** Keep up with market news, economic data, and industry trends that can impact your options strategies.
- **Read Books and Articles:** There's always more to learn about options. Explore books, articles, and educational resources from reputable sources.
- **Practice with Paper Trading:** Paper trading allows you to test your options strategies in a simulated environment without risking real capital.
- **Seek Guidance (Optional):** Consider learning from experienced options traders or mentors who can provide valuable insights and guidance.

Moving Forward

You now possess a solid foundation in options trading concepts. Remember, the key to success lies in applying your knowledge, managing risk effectively, and continuously learning and refining your approach.

Here are some steps to take action:

- **Develop a Trading Plan:** Craft a personalized trading plan that outlines your risk tolerance, investment goals, and preferred options strategies.
- **Start Small and Paper Trade:** Begin with smaller positions and practice paper trading to solidify your understanding and build confidence.
- **Monitor and Adjust:** Regularly monitor your options positions and be prepared to adjust your strategy as market conditions or your personal circumstances evolve.

Embrace the Challenge, Enjoy the Process

Options trading presents both challenges and rewards. Remember, the journey itself is an opportunity for learning and growth. By approaching options trading with a disciplined mindset, a commitment to risk management, and a thirst for continuous learning, you can navigate the market with greater confidence and potentially achieve your financial goals.

This concludes our options trading guide. Remember, the options market offers a vast and exciting landscape. So, equip yourself with the knowledge, manage risk wisely, and embark on your options trading adventure with a spirit of exploration and continuous learning.

Good luck!

APPENDIX

Glossary

This glossary provides a quick reference for key terms encountered throughout this options trading guide.

- **Underlying Asset:** The security (stock, ETF, etc.) on which an option contract is based.
- **Call Option:** The right, but not the obligation, to buy a specific underlying asset at a predetermined price (strike price) by a certain expiry date.
- **Put Option:** The right, but not the obligation, to sell a specific underlying asset at a predetermined price (strike price) by a certain expiry date.
- **Strike Price:** The predetermined price at which you can buy (call option) or sell (put option) the underlying asset.
- **Expiry Date:** The date by which you must exercise your option to buy or sell the underlying asset.
- **Premium:** The cost of purchasing an option contract.

- **Intrinsic Value:** The difference between the current market price of the underlying asset and the strike price (for in-the-money options only).
- **Time Value:** The remaining time until the option expires (plays a larger role for options closer to expiry).
- **Assignment:** The process by which a call option seller is obligated to sell the underlying asset or a put option buyer is obligated to buy the underlying asset upon exercise of the option.
- **Covered Call:** An options strategy where you sell a call option while already owning the underlying asset, limiting potential gains but generating income from the premium received.
- **Cash-Secured Put:** An options strategy where you sell a put option while depositing cash as collateral, potentially generating income from the premium received while limiting potential downside risk.
- **Bull Call Spread:** An options strategy involving buying a call option with a lower strike price and selling a call option with a higher strike price on the

same underlying asset, limiting potential gains but offering some downside protection compared to a naked call option.

- **Bear Put Spread:** An options strategy involving selling a call option with a lower strike price and buying a call option with a higher strike price on the same underlying asset, limiting potential profits but potentially gaining from a decline in the stock price.
- **Butterfly Spread:** A multi-leg options strategy involving buying and selling options contracts with different strike prices on the same underlying asset, aiming to profit from a limited price movement in the stock.
- **Straddle:** An options strategy involving buying both a call option and a put option with the same strike price on the same underlying asset, profiting from significant price movements in either direction.
- **Strangle:** An options strategy involving buying a call option and a put option with different strike prices on the same underlying asset, profiting from significant price movements in either direction.

- **Delta (Δ):** A measure of how much an option's price will change for every $1 change in the underlying stock price.
- **Gamma (Γ):** A measure of how quickly the Delta itself changes.
- **Rho (P):** A measure of how sensitive an option's price is to changes in interest rates.
- **Moving Average (MA):** An indicator that smooths out price fluctuations by averaging a stock's price over a specific period.
- **Relative Strength Index (RSI):** An indicator that measures a stock's recent price movements to gauge whether it is oversold or overbought.
- **Bollinger Bands (BB):** A set of upper and lower bands around a moving average, which expand and contract based on the stock's price volatility.
- **Support Level:** A price area where the stock price tends to find buying interest and bounce back up.
- **Resistance Level:** A price area where the stock price tends to face selling pressure and may be rejected.

This glossary provides a foundational understanding of options terminology. Remember, ongoing learning is crucial in the options market. Explore additional resources to deepen your knowledge and confidently navigate your options trading journey.

BONUS

Practice Exercises and Sample Trading Plans

You have grasped the fundamental concepts of options trading. But before risking real capital, it is vital to solidify your understanding and practice applying your knowledge. This section provides practice exercises and sample trading plans to help you refine your options strategy and build confidence through paper trading.

Practice Exercises:

- **Scenario Analysis:** Test your understanding of options by analyzing hypothetical scenarios. Identify the appropriate options strategy (covered call, cash-secured put, etc.) based on the market outlook and desired outcome.

- **Option Pricing:** Practice calculating the theoretical value of options contracts using tools like option pricing calculators or online resources. This hones your understanding of factors impacting option prices.
- **Paper Trading Simulations:** Simulate real-world trading using paper trading platforms. These platforms allow you to execute options trades without risking real capital. Experiment with different strategies, track your performance, and refine your approach based on the results.

Sample Trading Plans:

Template 1: Conservative Income Generation

- **Goal:** Generate consistent income through options strategies.
- **Risk Tolerance:** Low
- **Options Strategy:** Cash-Secured Puts
- **Underlying Assets:** Focus on blue-chip stocks with a history of stable dividends.
- **Strike Price:** Choose a put option with a strike price slightly below the current market price.

- **Expiry Date:** Select expiry dates 30-45 days out to balance time value and potential income generation. But for weekly income generation, select 5 days expiry date.
- **Position Sizing:** Allocate a small percentage (e.g., 5%) of your capital per trade.
- **Exit Strategy:** Close the position when the premium income reaches a predetermined target or if the stock price nears the strike price.

Template 2: Bullish Stock Outlook with Defined Risk

- **Goal:** Profit from a potential rise in the stock price while limiting downside risk.
- **Risk Tolerance:** Moderate
- **Options Strategy:** Bull Call Spread
- **Underlying Assets:** Stocks with a positive long-term outlook but potential for short-term volatility.
- **Strike Prices:** Choose a call option with a lower strike price (slightly in-the-money or at-the-money) and sell a call option with a higher strike price.

- **Expiry Date:** Select expiry dates that align with your anticipated timeframe for the stock price to rise.
- **Position Sizing:** Allocate a moderate percentage (e.g., 10%) of your capital per trade.
- **Exit Strategy:** Close the position when the stock price reaches your target profit level or if the outlook for the stock changes.

These are just samples. You should customize your trading plan based on your individual goals, risk tolerance, and market conditions.

Here is a table summarizing the two sample trading plans discussed previously:

Feature	Conservative Income Generation (Cash-Secured	Bullish Stock Outlook with Defined Risk (Bull Call

	Puts)	Spread)
Goal	Generate consistent income	Profit from potential stock price rise with limited downside risk
Risk Tolerance	Low	Moderate
Options Strategy	Cash-Secured Put	Bull Call Spread
Underlying Assets	Blue-chip stocks with stable dividend history	Stocks with positive long-term outlook, potential short-term volatility
Strike Price (Put)	Slightly below	Lower strike price

	current market price	(slightly in-the-money or at-the-money)
Strike Price (Call)	N/A	Higher strike price
Expiry Date	30-45 days out or 5 days for weekly options	Aligned with anticipated timeframe for stock price rise
Position Sizing	Small percentage of capital (e.g., 5%)	Moderate percentage of capital (e.g., 10%)
Exit Strategy	Close when premium reaches target or stock	Close when target profit reached or stock outlook

	nears strike price	changes

Sample Trading Plans

We strongly encourage paper trading before risking real capital.

Here is why:

- **Safe Learning Environment:** Experiment with different options strategies without financial consequences.
- **Develops Confidence:** Build your skills and gain confidence in your decision-making before entering the live market.
- **Tests Your Trading Plan:** Evaluate the effectiveness of your trading plan in a simulated environment.

By dedicating time to practice exercises and paper trading, you will be well-equipped to navigate the options market with greater confidence and potentially achieve your financial goals. So, grab a paper trading platform, experiment with different strategies, and refine your approach before taking the leap into the real world of options trading.

ABOUT THE AUTHOR

Dr. M. D. Lloyd is a passionate financial educator and options trading strategist with extensive experience in the financial markets. Dr. Lloyd's academic background (denoted by the Ph.D.) combined with his practical knowledge equips him to explain complex options concepts in a clear and accessible manner.

Driven by a desire to empower individuals to take control of their financial futures, Dr. Lloyd has dedicated his career to financial education and helping others navigate the options market with confidence. This book is a culmination of that passion, providing readers with a practical guide to unlock the potential of options trading and achieve their financial goals.

www.ingramcontent.com/pod-product-compliance
Lightning Source LLC
Chambersburg PA
CBHW082206220526
45470CB00010B/3069